T0113671

stem of the moon

Thandi Sliepen

Published in 2021 by Modjaji Books
Cape Town, South Africa

www.modjajibooks.co.za

© Thandi Sliepen

Cover artwork 'boy and the moon', 1994 by Thandi Sliepen

Edited by Arja Salfranca
Book layout by Andy Thesen
Set in Garamond
Printed and bound by Digital Action, Cape Town
ISBN print: 978-1-928433-31-6
ISBN ebook: 978-1-928433-33-0

if you are walking in a garden
and the sun is weighing you down
wait for the night
you can lean on the stem
of the moon

Dedicated to Glen Green and the twenty-three
gentle years we had together.

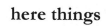

here things

ten cents

the children
like butterflies
are out after the rain
swarming down the streets
fluttering and begging for fruit

all day white butterflies
have come from the northwest
from the direction of the rain and wind
where the sun sets
in winter

in this river of life
are the young always
hatched downstream
forever does the current run and none
lays its eggs where it begun

the children
like butterflies
are flowing through the town
standing outside doors and shops
for rands and ten cents

silent witnesses
to passing wealth and summer
waiting in the wings
or pouring forth
after the rain

chile our madman

is carefully walking
around the village square
as if examining
his own personal gift

as if it were laid out just so
in design and perspective
for his pleasure
that he might delight
in observing its ways

blue sweatshirt
knobbly knees
hands buttoned into pockets
of flared schoolboy shorts
chile travels distant lands each day
around this
our square

while the town bustles and revolves
in its own orbit
tourists flock the shops
to buy stones
unhappy children trailing
unhappy parents
holding up the stones
exclaiming

they have found it
what they always wanted
all their lives
they depart carrying their weights
driving away in expensive shells
past the curio shops

past chile and his precious feet
and beard turning snow white
beneath him
with the seasons the green trees
in the square turn to dust

chile wears his torn beige coat all winter
over his blue sweatshirt
as the cars skate
around the square

petrus

perched on his mealie meal
on his *sucrus*
and *saltis* he said

gleefully lounging on a wheelbarrow
swinging his legs full of mirth
raising his palms to the sky

full of mirth when i ask
where do you get
your water ?

wouda

i see you animated
listing colours
prussian blue
viridian
magenta
payne's grey
saying how you would never
use black again

i remember your paintings
of ships of fools
i remember you
on a bar stool

old bethlehem car guard

the art of willing away time
cheerfully
the dance of loud small talk
refined nods
swaying while standing
a gnarled supple human tree
planted
in a car park

black snow

there is a man
on the burnt earth
a grey pep store blanket
cape flowing in the wind
a man hoarding wood
on unsteady drunk-like legs

when he sleeps he wraps
himself in his blanket
under the church sky
the burnt earth
the darker patches
on the dark land

when the man walks
through the night
he ruffles the townsfolk
asleep in their beds
the burnt veld below his feet
crunching
like black snow

when he passes
lopsided muttering
he leaves a wake of dreams
a slurry of odd planks and beams
carrying off parts of people's burdens
like some kind of pep store christ

the night makes way for his passage
a kind of keeling ship
ash turns to snow
and ushers
him through

artist's cafe

trees wrapped in red crimplene
adults wrapped in coffee and holidays
free time
and sunshine in a small town

a playground of repurposed implements
on the verge of the square
old faces waiting
for the children

saturday sounds

a sea of sound breaking
from the township below
funeral harmonies
popping disco beats
a reedy lesiba
a man calling
come come come
let's go

this garden is blossoming waves
human flower voices
bells and hooter bees weaving
into the caves of my ears
a surge of splashing children
somewhere out there
diving headlong
into the afternoon

washing up a lone child
into this garden
rubbing his stomach
my face like stone
i ask him do you sniff glue?
his face stops
he clutches his head no
he clutches his throat no

then his face lights up
he says do you know nina?
tell her christian says hello
he asks do you remember me?
do you know manthithi?
his face shines
and becomes a child's face

the stone from my own
cracks and crashes to the ground

i ask where do you live?
he points
there by the donga
how many of you?
three and grandmother
miesies
don't call me miesies i shout
from a long long way away
over the veld
between the sighing leaves
it trails into my ears
i hear him whisper
thandi he whispers
thandi

the girl on the planet

when too much matter
skin and detail has dragged on
i go with the clot of confusion
to visit the girl
on the planet

whatever new things you bring
you may forget
the girl on the planet can choose
to see only the ball she stands on
that is all
rejoice
the circus tent is darkened
she is not looking at the paying crowded faces
she is standing in an illuminated
round room

where one day on the white walls
she saw all the rooms she had ever been in
and was yet to be in
like a row of lanterns
like a necklace of glowing beads
running over her collarbones
behind her neck
to where she could not see

rejoice
she is standing on the roof of africa
watching a full moon
a round headed flower
climbing into the sky
a swaying
cobra ladder

and she has noticed
she is not alone
that all are standing equally
on the planet

and when masses upon masses
of people came
almost too many for the planet to support
she saw so many faces
and that miraculously
she was still standing

there were now just
more feet
blossoming from the planet
were doing various acrobatics
in the sand
and she thought she had never
felt so well expressed

here things

a tapestry of clouds
hangs behind the dam
a tapestry of hues
for blue

i float on the dam
a suspended watery hammock
strung between
the mountains

the sun's sequins overlapping
on the walls of my eyes
i turn like a windmill
on a breath of wind

or like a compass needle
idling
homing in on my own
true direction

i walk through the veld
past an abandoned farmhouse
a remnant pear tree
a bonfire of white blossoms still lit every spring

i climb the mountain
along its seams collecting pieces of the earth's
agate veins in my hands like broken pipettes
where life once ran through

i glide over sandstone promenades
with good light on the lichen
to my eyrie of stone
that perfectly fits the curve of my back

that has perhaps become my backbone
i watch ants roam
like the living walking particles
of sandstone

i meander in the valleys
and splash
over pink willow roots
carpeting shallow streams

past wattle and daub ruins
wafers of clay you can count
like the rings of trees
vibrant settlements of not so long ago

and then back home
down a lane lined with lombardy poplars
red and gold candles melting
with the seasons

past one of those old billboards
that used to say
discover your soul
visit the free state

shell song

catastrophe

i am like a shellfish wedged between
mother of pearl mirrors
the ocean to me seems a catastrophe
see how i hug the pearly gates
and retreat
see how i sleep recoiled
from the sea that seems
a shock to me
existence brushes my surfaces
throwing her salty arms around my neck
probing for my salty heart

the edge of remembering
and forgetting
holds me in her watery gaze
my viscous horizon
see how well i have slept
for the world seemed
a catastrophe

kelp forest

dreams surface like butterfish
gliding between the folds
of our minds leaving a wake
of phosphorescent foam

sleep like tides taking you out
each breath pulling you into her depths
sucking you from the shore
carrying you further than you remember
being before

the sea the great store house of the unknown
where possibilities are served
from the deep dream body
behind the counter of the intertidal zone
where we come to receive
what we need

go lightly
with the surging heartbeat
through the kelp forest
where the currents weave
and the kelp leaves glissade
between the rocks

the standing place

you are the rock
in this kaleidoscopic wonder
of swaying weed
darting fish
and wandering walking shells

you the rock
that caught my feet
gave me a footing
as i floated by
lost as a seed

you the rock
that i may feel the touch
of deep sea giants
brushing past
and not feel afraid

that i may hear
the loud breathing
of the shore
and not close my ears
to my own heartbeat

and when i grow old
rock and my long leaves
are tattered
or after a violent storm
i will be washed up

look then
for the light on the surface
that will always reflect
your face
my rock of ages

oysters

there is a girl on the wild coast
peeling oysters
sparkling blue sea
opaque shells
the bright light palms of the girl
darting between the chunky oyster homes
levering them open with a screwdriver
with a translucent
orange handle

the women are diving for crayfish
bobbing between the rocks like seals
hugging the shore with padded soaked clothes
and gloved hands
short matted hair glistening
full female bodies
round seal eyes
looking out of the ocean

while their young daughters recline
on the shore like mermaids
combing the sand with their fingers
into wide hooped sand skirts
like two halves of a fruit
a sea fruit universe radiating out from a core
warm sand grains fanned and aligned
by mermaids at home
in the great divide

shell song

my mother comes towards me
holding shells
in her hands
in her hands
for me

my mother comes towards me
holding shells
in her hands
and asks me to choose
my favourite ones
to me
for me

my mother says the shells
are like poems
some more beautiful
than the rest

positive

i am sheltering in a white room
in the ablutions
where moths rest in silence

outside the winds howl
breaking like surf on the trees
tapping and rocking our shells

in my mother of pearl room
all is tranquil and secure
in this room where dreams are expelled

where mirrors watch
time drips and moths
hold their tongues

from this white cavern
i call
from the rock of my throat

from the peace in my heart
i hear the call of the ocean
and my chance to answer

like waves entering a sea cave
salt water
is etching my womb

my body open to sea
the sky
and the roar of life

poem to an unborn child

we are resting next to a half-built castle
balanced on the rim
of a mountain

we have been terribly shaken getting here
the castle a ruin of human folly
half-built fantasies
treacherous staircases
gaping pits
and windows with nowhere to stand
to look out of

from this high sandstone plateau
i see the undulating land before me
from every angle the perfect stage
the perfect host the perfect mirror
the enduring land
our faithful friend that stays behind
every time we leave
and welcomes us
each time we return

the land's arms endlessly open
like your father's lips puckered and ready
when i quietly re-enter the house
after a dawn meditation
as if he has been lying there forever
waiting for me
the patient earth
all the shadows
all the memories

gatekeeper

i am like a gatekeeper
my body the portal
you the wayfarer
the one i have been waiting for
the one for whom
i have been manning this gate

i am like a tree
anticipating a storm
before the wind
i stand still
i cannot walk out
and meet the wind

when the storm comes
i will quake
when it passes
i will stand still again
only richer
with you

precipice

these last few days
with you still hidden
from our eyes
the face of mystery
screened behind swirling red veils
shifting in the dark breeze

while i hover
on the edge of a precipice
on the other side
is me
holding you in my arms
i cannot see across this chasm

in labour with you

my man asleep on the maternity bed
while i walk corridors courted by pain
a fleeting visitor who casts a shadow over us
our heartbeats speed up as our visitor arrives
a visitor that could arrive
at any time in our lives

if i could i would have us at home
all this while
and not in this hospital edifice
home where we could have welcomed our guest
with familiar trees and wind
but i see life has arranged
a different venue

a stark room that hums with artificial light
hallways that lead past rooms of bleeding
bare-breasted women
a glass room with premature babies
clinging to life like dehydrated bats
in transparent boxes
tunnels that end in dimmed swinging doors
leading onto other illuminated realms

i find my way back
to this pale flickering room
our friend pain waiting
for surely we will be friends
before this night is through
as we emerge into sun
after all these tunnels

for does pain not visit us all
across this earth
so we can feel each other
so we can reach each other
across our manifold divides
a bridge to treasure
for it brings me
closer to thee

berthed

the wind makes you smile
you arrived like a ship in full blast
a lone white bird rounding
the peninsular of my harbour
the ship i longed for
for so long
will you stay awhile?

and in these early days of refurbishing
fitting out of a new façade
new sails
and the cleaning of hulls
i wonder how long will we sail together
will i stay awhile?

outside the harbour
wind tears
and the sky is streaked in foam
yet we dream of new lands
a calm blue expanse
we are setting sail and the wind
still makes you smile

afresh

my son is examining his hands
as if they are planes
or butterflies
he has just caught on the ends
of his new green tendrils
toes like pink sea anemones
radiating out into the world

to catch you from the depths
and name you afresh
your fontanelle like the skin of some deep
beating drum
pulsing beneath my finger tapping
a single lock of hair

my cooing turtle dove
my baby long-nosed monkey
just today discovering
your hair

oh when your hands are bare
and they move
through the air

the ladybirds are in the apricot trees

your ancient owl eyes

watching me
upside down

when you pointed
your theodolite
to the mountain
i saw the cairn hanging
from the bottom
of the moon

the fabled land

to come upon each other
at the end of the millennium
at midnight on a crowded
dance floor

drawn together by opportune tides
with four seconds to spare
we clasp each other
with wonder at our good fortune

like two ships
rafted alongside each other
on a turbulent
midnight sea

you surprised me
like this life
that rose from the darkness
from a depth unseen

and those floating islands of land
i dreamt we climbed together
those hovering
golden koppies

the fabled land
it is here now
with four seconds
to spare

in the garden of the gods

in the veld with a man and a dog
and a stream running
through our kitchen
to imagine you must be in heaven
what a surprise
to find you are in heaven

and then to wake
with the dog almost sleeping
on your head
to feel angry and realise
you cannot be in heaven
quite yet

in the garden of the gods
submerged in a sandstone bed
observing from the eye of noon
looking out of the urn of existence
mortar and pestle rock pools
your body ground between sun and stone

and a cave to call home
for a night
to feel as if you belong
on the earth and that is why
you call it heaven

in the playground of the gods
a family of donkeys frolicking
on the hillside
laughing doves
laughing
from the cabbage trees

motouleng cave

our oldest room
lightening lights her mouth
hands drum her chest
ash plasters
her bones

cave of dreams
deep overhang of stone
conscious hollow beneath a petrified desert
a balcony in the bend of a river
that flows on and on

motouleng awake
for as long as there have been ears
to hear her
people to paint her
soot and laughter

bubbling voices
dreaming and asking
to remember the future
on the shoulders
of the past

candles flicker
in the recesses
bald ibis roost in the roof
from our oldest chamber
to the latest wing

motouleng
to give thanks
to clap our hands
to clap our wings
to clap our hearts

the ladybirds are in the apricot trees

the cats are purring like tractors
the crickets ringing their bicycle bells
summer like a bandwagon you can catch a lift
in the direction you are going

at home the ladybirds are in the apricot trees
nestled between stems and warm fruit
ladybirds with surprising combinations
of black and red

and wings tucked away like secret sails
hurriedly unclipped in the hot breeze
our harvest of sunlight
highveld years

days like washing hung out to dry
my heart a station
i have disembarked
in the free state

where am i except in
a room in god's mind
fingerprint clouds
pressed to the sky

at home it is high summer
a torrent of seeds overflowing
onto the moist nursery soil
a brown jug pouring green

golden jubilee tomatoes
black prince
your balls like sweet ripe figs
full of seeds

my body
like an avocado pear
creamy
and rich

and just like flesh
around a seed
our bodies will fall away
and rot

and all that will remain
is this kernel
we grew
you and me

the clay beneath our fingernails
and streaming
through our veins
will be remoulded

our minds
cast off
and the mountains
will absorb our faces

and pegged poems
pegged to the land
will just remain poems
poems that were carefully unfolded

and laid out on a patch of earth
my life a tattered blanket
with the veld
poking through

my lover beside me
imprinting his kiss
programming my soul
imparting new directions home

autumn sun

coming further and further
inside
a tinkling in a forgotten room
my nose like an old cave
registering change
autumn a time to find out
if your chimney is blocked

the ants are pouring out of the walnuts
like fountains
barnacles on our pumpkins
grown from the nibbles
of rodents
pumpkins i carry home
like a golden carriage in my skirt

namibia

dead pan

i will meet you at
dead pan
love

when we are long gone
we will meet in the moonlight
and once again in the snow
but leave no footprints this time
as we go

epupa

how many feet have followed
this path along epupa falls
a powdery track on a glassy cliff
a scrambling passage alongside the pounding
footfalls of the kunene river
as it separates into a thousand gorges
a million milky fans

gatekeeper baobabs lean
over every stream
as if in an old japanese print
a waterfall in perfection
that sounds like a million
hands clapping

overhead the autumn hills are dotted
with amber trees naively painted
fish eagles pierce the light
and young girls gather
to try and plait your hair
their delighted fingers feel
like a wave of ants
rustling your mind

while in the pools by the palms
the boys are bathing
airing their blankets

the women washing further out
on the shoulders of the falls
scrubbing their skin
lathering clothes

in their open air bathroom
busy with their toilette
on the lip of epupa

as the river pours past
out of angola like cream
past a flock of fat-tailed sheep
and lithe shepherds
with their horns of hair
past a donkey contemplating
the pink sands downstream

spitzkoppe

another island on the
plains another
nurturing stone mother
boulders and breasts
these women sit all over africa
oases of stone
portals in the night where wisdom
flows out
like a warm desert breeze

her body shifts
her face traces the ever
travelling orbs of light
she whispers
only i will remember
that you were ever here

lekhubu island

the winds blow off the salt pans
autumn leaves clatter on the quartz
the warm winds caress
the old pumpkin skins of the baobabs
arms stiffly out they stand
like stuffed toys or balloons
blown up from their bases
or giant potatoes that grew out into the universe
with cream of tartar moons

lekhubu where butterflies kiss your lips
red beetles comb your feet
and moths come to drink from your body at night
with purple-eyed wings
where you remember half-formed dreams
and wake to share an instant with beings
who have stood in one place for centuries
seldom venturing out further
than their shadows

the great baobabs stand on a crystal island
in a dry brittle sea
cloaked in elephant hide with a rose blush
shimmering roots in space
dark lands hover like dark birds on the horizon
where you can walk out
onto the pale crusty pan and
it's like walking on
meringue

chobe

elephant bones scattered
like knuckle bones
from a mighty soothsayer's hand

who can tell the paths
and ways of fortune through
the mopane trees
for these heavy walkers
on the life line

who leave behind soft bevelled bowls
in the sand and skulls
like enormous porous shells
or marble termite halls
perfect headstones
under the trees
when all the rest have gone

the himba

women with children
hanging like ripening fruit
on their bodies
dripping from a red earth tree

women shaking milk
in their hives
or under a canopy outside
beneath a halo of flies

budding girls prance with soft doe eyes
shaded by ears of plaited hair
like newborn goats flirting
with the new world

himba with your third shoulder blade of iron
bound to the earth
with metal weights to keep you
from floating away

the village comes alive
after dark
the himba like elves
gathered around twinkling firelights

goat bladder fairy crowns
lead and leather
you feel safe
in those dry lands

stones

my son is throwing stones into the kunene river
the joy of throwing little stones
and big ones too
into the massive epupa falls
which we hear is still
to be dammed

my son with his himba necklace
and rainbow hat
sizing up all the children
crowded curiously around him
then back to the serious work
of plugging up the falls with stones

quiver tree

wrapped in gold foil
stars like decorations
hung on the ends of your arms
branches that rise like smooth
grey umbilical cords
into the sky

kokerboom
alive you stand before me
in a landscape of crystal fountains
your succulent leaves course overhead
over quartz outcrops that peel off layers
in the sun like lizards

choje when you die
you stand before me empty
with no one
in the darkened doorway
your limbs once ran through
the exact constellation
you followed
where you pinned your stars
and left them hanging

odd shards of life

mangosteen moon

afar a fragile segment floats
tender and moist
in the protective shell of the sky
gecko calls out its name
frog loudly knocks
while crickets scrape the teeth
of their combs rhythmically
tapping on night's door

at dusk white herons
alight on the trees lining the streets
of their chosen people
dogs retire to the temples
and babies are born
with bells on their new feet

women thread fishes
and men build bamboo towers
or remain reposed in courtyards
like frangipani trees
with twisted arms in the ruins of time

in this land of white-fleshed fruits
and flowers like bright bird's beaks
where doves lilt
though they may be snared and sold
in this time of the birds
though they may be in cages

in the assembling darkness
a procession pours out onto the sand
a river of flags and parasols
the pilgrim's offerings a mountain

on the shore like a bonfire
for a passing ship

the gamelan orchestra strikes up between our bones
stars watch the drama
on earth island
while out to sea the fishermen
in their handmade jukung
are turning their prows to dawn
when their nets will catch only light

conch shell prayer

the blessed rope
of life leading us through
the night like
the holy infant in our arms
like the silver reins
of our golden chariots
as we skim the clouds
like flying fish

the blessed rope of life
in a cosmic tug of war
the forces balanced
yet the centre fragile
the struggle cuts deeper
into our hands
than i could have
imagined

the tower

i remember this stone lane
these canals where swans drift
like pure white jugs
floating pitchers in the streams

the stone steps
under my feet like pedals
the windows along the way
fields of crimson and yellow

streamers of old floral cloth
hang like curtains in the dappled light
the bright flags accompany
me from tree to tree

past clearings of ragged crows
nativity sheep
and fields where muscular horses
stand with flared feet

their sturdy foals newly arrived
gazing out of tender eyes
fields of crimson and yellow
on either side

down the cobblestone corridor
lined with oak trees i cycle
down the green alley looking
out of oak windows

a blur of passing fields
a bunch of flowers
crimson and yellow
in my hand

the cobblestones
a staircase of woven
pink bricks
i tread full of hope

garland prayer

lord please take all the beads
of my life
beads i have turned in my fingers
like leaves
pages
falling
crumpled veins
red and gold
spilling from my fingers

please take all the beads of my life
and gather them in your hands
these odd shards of life
these smooth wooden beads
shuffle and scatter
these serpents of glitter coiled
around my feet
i would break the spell
of the spinning wheel

i would thread my brightest beads
and garland your willow branches
amber heart
i believe
you weave garlands
from even
the oddest shards

autumn lane

the cracks of sunlight in the trees
have turned to pools
of red leaves
they hang like butterflies
wings pirouetting
a final lover's embrace
with the wind

they fall like stars
on the cobblestones
dusting the purple bricks
fluttering below my feet
like spent wishes i have no need
of them

at the end of the day

swallow

trapped in the white house
all these days of drought
the girl child brought you to me
as if i would know
what to do
with her special gift

all day i worked sculpting
shaded under the walnut trees
towards evening you opened your eyes
lifted your innermost lid
unblinking
to see the world pass

swallow in my hand
i can still feel the gentle tap
of your heartbeat
on my palm
or now
just my own

swallow with a winged tail
crescent arms and an emerald sheen
in the light
come to teach me
about the moment
we all share

atlantic giant

sits on my stoep
the universe
on my stoep in the body
of a pumpkin

delicate laced web
longitudes and latitudes
you can trace
with your fingers

but what i love most
about our pumpkin
universe
is that it has a stem

moth song

when mama was moth
and our dusty wings
everywhere

when she held our hand
and flew to the moon
there was only light
when mama was moth

stem of the moon

if you are walking in a garden
and the sun is weighing you down
wait for the night
you can lean on the stem of the moon

she rises like an ethereal flower
between the silver trees
floating on dark waters
a shimmering beam

through the balm of the night
she arrives
like a pathway
a glowing bridge

my breath on dormant moths
stirring them to life
night piecing me
together

from the crush of the day
people so fragile and far
we barely brush each other
with our tendril arms

the sun evaporating
and reforming us like clouds
carded and rearranged
in the absorbent air

we are names in the wind
as children we hold visions in our hands
later they are lost
in pockets

seemingly forgotten
in our flood-lit sky
how we forget her bloom
and poison her root

yet she reaches out
like a kite in our hands
we may gather-in more string
and more and more

until we are there
and the earth
has become a precious
blue flower in our hands

time overgrown

farmhouses that once kept us warm
windows
we once looked out of elated
at the falling snow

have turned into holes
breezy gaps
ruins we can now step through

surrender hill
settled like the past
those dried roses still gathering dust
in the turret tower

your beloved

a portal to pour
your love out into space
a windmill creaking and turning in the veld
your love fanning out
through a window
in the wind

veld

that has clothed me like my skin
like its very own
has told me
we are of the same fabric

to find heaven
on earth is to join your being
to the land
wherever you may find it

like a shellfish
finding a suitable rock
to fasten your heart
onto the surface of existence

radiant earth
may we find
our place
on your body

the region we attire
the part we play
may we embrace you
warmly

epitaph song

fleeting cast shadow
turned her face
and smiled
as the truth of time
played and danced on her life
and she said
your nature is free
you're not written on stone
not like this tombstone

fleeting cast shadow
turned her face
and she smiled
as the truth of time
played and danced on her life
and she said your nature is clear
poured from life's own pure jug
you're not written in stone
not like this tombstone

fleeting cast shadow
watched the sun go down
she saw the procession of shadows
passing over the land
and she said your nature must grow
and let go
of all that you know

you're written
in snow
freshly falling snow

lieve mama

you taught me
how my mother glides
you filled the shoes
and steps
of my mother's dance
you spread your wings
and flew
always towards harmony
ageing mama you show me
the changing face
of my mother

your arms surround me
like a sun-filled valley
lambs bask on the slopes
tall grasses sway
lulling me to sleep
in this warm room
your patient eyes the sun and moon
watch over my cradle
and nourish my infant arms
reaching out
to follow your light

at the end of the day

at the end of the day do we weigh
every grain of sand
as it pours through our hands
no
we just let them go

at the end of the day do we wake
to the sound of bells
distant cow bells tinkling
or the peel of church bells
yes
and a wisp of a melody
turtle doves and flutes
somewhere in our room

at the end of the day
do we rise to a cacophony of frogs
and answering jackals
rise with the last quarter of the moon
to realise
you were always a shell and the fruit
is vibrating and rejoicing within you
that you will discard the shell
presently

at the end of the day
are we like rivers that broaden
as we approach the ocean
silent travellers in the night
flowing out of the prison gates
an expanded flooded mother
a sheet of tranquillity
tilting out towards
the beckoning surf

do we hear only sea
as we let go of land
and everything that once held us fast
the beloved land
that sifted each drop
as it fell
from the mystery

shore song

what will you do
when you reach the shore
what will you do
when you get home
tell me what will you do
with the time

i'll labour and toil
and turn the soil
i guess i'll always be planting seeds
i'll plant and watch
them grow

Glossary

Chobe: A national park in northern Botswana.

Choje: The indigenous San name for the quiver tree.

Donga: A dry gully caused by the action of water erosion.

Epupa: A waterfall on the Kunene river on the border of Angola and Namibia.

Gamelan: Traditional Indonesian ensemble music, predominantly of percussion instruments.

Himba: The Himba, or OvaHimba, are indigenous peoples living in northern Namibia and southern Angola.

Kokerboom: Afrikaans name for the quiver tree.

Kunene: A river that flows from the Angolan highlands south to the border with Namibia.

Lekhubu: A rock outcrop in the Makgadigadi region of the Sua Pan, the largest pan in Botswana.

Lesiba: Traditional mouth-blown, single-stringed musical instrument of the Basotho.

Lieve: Dutch word for dear, as in writing letters. Also a Dutch female name.

Mangosteen: A tropical fruit from Southeast Asia.

Miesies: A name that a servant (usually black) calls a white female employer in South Africa.

Motouleng: Largest overhang cave in the southern hemisphere. Sacred cave in the eastern Free State. Also known as the fertility cave, place of beating drums. Name described to author as 'the sound of hands clapping, to give thanks'.

Spitzkoppe: A group of granite peaks or inselbergs in the Namib Desert.

Thandi Sliepen is a self-taught painter, sculptor, poet and gardener living in Ladybrand in the Free State with her two children.

Born in 1971 in Mowbray Cape Town she left South Africa in 1976 and eventually settled with her family in New Zealand.

Thandi returned to South Africa in 1991 and has been based predominantly in the Free State ever since.

Recently Thandi opened an small art gallery hA_dE_dA gallery in her home in Ladybrand and built a cob house in her garden 'the Mill' – an earthen abode where she grinds wheat for herself and locals and which also doubles as an unusual Airbnb experience. A sunny 'artist's cottage' full of local art work is also in the garden and available for accommodation.

Though involved in many art forms Thandi says poetry was her first love.

Printed in the United States
by Baker & Taylor Publisher Services